painting on ceramics

painting on ceramics

KATE BYRNE

Photography by Sandra Lane
Text by Suzannah Gough

CONTENTS

Introduction

Getting started

Projects & alternative designs

Templates & motifs

How to use this book

Painting on ceramics has become increasingly popular in recent years, not least because it is surprisingly easy and extremely rewarding to create professional-looking pieces with no previous experience. Once you become familiar with a few basic techniques and principles, you will be ready to explore an entire world of color and patternmaking. If this is your first creative endeavor, you will be delighted by the sense of achievement on completing your first piece. Many devotees of the craft also describe its therapeutic qualities.

This book provides eight projects with detailed step-by-step instructions for decorating different items of tableware. Along the way you will also learn a selection of techniques, from stenciling and mono-printing to using stamps and masking fluid. The projects will familiarize you with the fundamentals and will act as a springboard for your own ideas and designs.

While all the projects featured involve painting underglaze colors onto bisque, additional information is given to help you adapt the techniques for painting with acrylic on preglazed and fired ceramics. This will enable those of you who don't have access to a kiln to create designs that can be fired in a home oven.

Before you begin the projects, read and digest the information provided in the Getting Started section. This will introduce you to the basic equipment and methods, from choosing and using brushes to applying color and tracing motifs. Next, choose a project and read through the instructions so you understand them before you begin. It is also a good idea to practice the techniques on a scrap piece of bisque, glazed ceramics, or paper so you are more confident when it comes to painting the piece itself.

To give you even more choice, each project is accompanied by additional pages of alternative designs. Some of these use the same technique explained in the project, but there are also ideas for using techniques described elsewhere in the book. These should be used in tandem with the index, which will direct you to the relevant instructions.

Instead of simply explaining how to replicate my designs, I have also introduced each project with a brief explanation about how I arrived at the design. This should help you understand some basic design principles, such as how to choose colors or how to wrap a flat pattern over a three-dimensional object.

Finally, the Africa design used on the mug project is provided as an alternative design for all the projects so you can create a complete set of tableware.

Whether you have some experience in painting or are a complete novice, I hope this book will develop your confidence and inspire you to experiment with designing your own patterns and enjoying the creative process.

KATE BYRNE

LEFT *A selection of brushes and other equipment used for decorating ceramics, including a sgraffito tool.*

RIGHT *Paints for ceramics come in a variety of different forms. Powdered underglaze, shown here, is mixed with underglaze medium and diluted with water.*

Getting started

Surfaces for painting

This book provides all the information a beginner will need to decorate blank bisque, the name given to ceramics that have been fired but not yet glazed.

Bisque is available from a number of different sources. Pottery cafés, which have become very popular in recent years, provide a line of bisque, from cups and saucers to plates and large bowls, ready for decoration with colored underglazes (see page 96). Parttime adult education courses, pottery studios, and various other suppliers also provide bisque. Unfired clay, known as greenware, can also be painted with underglazes, but it is more fragile to handle.

Eight specific painting projects for bisque, together with countless ideas for variations, are featured in this book. Don't worry if you cannot find an object identical to those that I have used; it is easy to adapt my designs to fit similar shapes, and all the measurements given are approximate.

In some of the photographs of the various projects, you will notice that the bisque has been placed on a decorating wheel. Although not an essential piece of equipment, using a decorating wheel means you can turn the bisque around smoothly as you paint without your fingers touching the surface.

Glazing & firing bisque

When you have decorated your piece, you will need to pass it on to a professional who will apply a layer of glaze (usually clear) and then fire the bisque in a kiln. This process will set the underglaze color, making the finished piece durable, water-resistant, and smooth to the touch. Generally, this process will mean you can eat from the piece and machine-wash it, but it is always best to check the underglaze manufacturer's label first.

There are two projects featured here – the Candy Cup and Saucer and the Salt and Pepper Shakers – that require special glazing techniques. Full instructions for these techniques are provided on the relevant pages.

Painting glazed ceramics & firing in a home oven

With the exception of the Striped Noodle Set and the Salt and Pepper Shakers, all the techniques described in this book can be adapted to acrylic-painting on plain ceramics that are already glazed and fired. You may already have some glazed pieces at home, but, if not, they are widely available in general household stores and can be decorated with colored acrylic paint and fired in a home oven in a well-ventilated space. Do bear in mind that the painted areas should never come into contact with food, and always check the manufacturer's advice on the label. Accordingly, it is best to use these objects for decorative purposes only.

LEFT *The stripes on these pottery cylinders show how a color looks painted in one, two, or three layers. By placing the cylinders side by side or on top of each other, you can see at a glance how the different shades compare. The numbers indicate the paint code.*

PREVIOUS PAGE *Unglazed pottery, known as bisque, ready for painting.*

Using underglazes & acrylics

Brush-on underglazes

Traditionally, underglaze colors come as powder paints that are mixed with an underglaze medium and then diluted with water. Underglazes are also available in tubes, ready for diluting. By far the easiest to use, however, are pre-mixed underglazes that come in liquid form ready to paint directly onto the bisque.

Underglazes are available in a huge choice of colors, which can also be mixed to create your own shades. The underglaze is then usually covered with clear glaze and fired, intensifying the color. When choosing colors, it is therefore very important to select from a catalog or from glazed and fired samples; the color you see in the pot is a duller, grayer version of the final result. For this reason, the colors in the step-by-step photographs are paler than in the photograph of the finished piece. You can use as many colors as you like in your designs, but the more successful patterns will be restricted to a maximum of five; any more will be confusing, both to paint and to look at.

Underglaze pens, crayons, & pencils

Underglaze colors also come as pens, crayons, printing blocks or pads, and pencils, which are wonderful for drawing fine lines, outlines, adding detail, and writing. Be aware that with underglaze pens the color can blob at the beginning and end of each stroke.

Correcting mistakes

Small mistakes can be wiped off with a clean, damp cloth. If the underglaze has dried, gently scrape the mistake off with the tip of a sharp knife. Pale colors won't leave any trace at all, but you may find that darker colors will stain the bisque slightly.

If you have already painted large areas and want to start again completely, you will need to use a lot of water to clean off the underglaze, possibly immersing your bisque in water. If this is the case, your piece will need to dry out completely before you can begin again. This can take up to a day, so to speed up the process you could put the bisque in a home oven at 300°F/150°C for half an hour to an hour, depending on how wet the bisque is.

Finally, be careful not to glaze any part of the object that will come in direct contact with the kiln shelf, such as the foot rim of a bowl; it will weld to the kiln during the firing process. Clean these areas with a wet sponge first.

Painting with acrylics

Acrylic paint can be hardened in a home oven and are ideal for painting ordinary household tableware that has already been glazed and fired; you can even use acrylics on glass. For this reason, if you do not have access to a professional kiln, acrylics are a viable alternative to underglazes. With the exception of the Noodle Set and the Salt and Pepper Shakers, all the techniques can be adapted by referring to the notes for each project.

Unlike underglazes, acrylics do not need to be glazed and the colors won't change in the oven, so what you see in the jar is true to the finished result. It is safest to use non-toxic paints, and to use them for decorative purposes only or to paint areas that will not come in contact with food. For example, if you are painting a serving bowl, paint the outside only, keeping away from the rim. In all instances, you should check the manufacturer's directions.

Acrylics are not available in as extensive a choice of colors as underglazes, but they can be mixed to create an almost infinite variety of colors.

FAR LEFT *The leaf shapes on this plate show how colors appear when they overlap each other.*

BELOW *A gradation of color is achieved by increasing the number of layers of paint.*

The intensity will depend on how thickly the acrylic is applied; one layer will create a dense color, while the paint can be diluted to create a wash. If you are going to overlay colors, the first layer must be dry before the next is applied or the effect will be muddy. Designs can be marked with pencil, but the marks will not burn off as with kiln-firing, so paint over the lines or wipe them off. If you make a mistake, wipe off the acrylic while it is still wet or scrape it off with a sharp knife when it is dry. After you have finished painting, clean the brushes with hot, soapy water before the acrylic dries.

Fire in a home oven in a well-ventilated room, following the manufacturer's directions. This will probably be at a temperature of 325°F/170°C for 30–45 minutes.

Background effects

There are many different techniques that can be used for creating wonderful background effects. Some are beautiful enough to be left without further decoration, particularly if they are on small pieces such as tiles. However, they can all be used as backgrounds to a main design or combined with other techniques. For example, you could stencil motifs onto a wash background, or speckle-glaze half an object and mono-print the other half. Once you have experimented with background effects and the techniques on the next few pages, you will soon develop your own ideas and combinations.

1&4 Speckle glaze

This comes in premixed pots in a variety of colors and with different quantities and sizes of specks. Apply one to three coats to bisque, as you do with ordinary underglaze colors. Speckle-glaze colors cannot be mixed, nor are they available in acrylic.

2 Crackle glaze

Apply one coat as you would a clear glaze. When fired, the glaze will crackle and create a distressed effect. Paint acrylic paint (dark colors are the most effective) over the crackled glaze, making sure the color goes into the cracks. Wipe off any excess paint with a damp sponge. You can use ordinary acrylic paint, or oven-fired acrylic if you expect to wash the piece frequently. Crackle glaze is for decorative purposes only. If you use underglaze instead of acrylic paint, the piece will need to be refired.

3 Sponging

Sponging on underglaze will result in different effects, depending on the density of the sponge. It is best to use a rounded sponge without corners. Saturate it with underglaze, squeeze off the excess, then gently dab the sponge onto the surface. Repeat with a second layer, if necessary, or add another color.

5 Underglaze crayons

Underglaze crayons can be used for a number of free-style effects. Try scribbling lines zigzag fashion, as shown, or experiment with other effects such as cross-hatching and stripes. For softer lines, smudge with your fingers. For the Salt and Pepper Shakers (see page 76), this technique was combined with a speckle glaze.

6 Spattering

You can use a stiff brush such as a toothbrush to load the underglaze and then flick it carefully onto the bisque. This method can be used on a plain white or colored underglaze background.

7 Wash

A wash is created by diluting the underglaze with water, resulting in a less intense color. Apply with a wide brush.

8 Matte underglaze

Some underglaze colors do not need to be glazed; when they are fired, the color remains dull and flat. This surface quality works particularly well in combination with glazed areas where the color intensifies and the surface is shiny. In the Candy Cup and Saucer project (see page 58), I left the bottom half of the cup unglazed to create a matte effect to contrast with the glazed top half. You could also leave areas of a design matte by masking out, then glazing (see also **10** and **11** on page 19).

Direct techniques

One of the pleasures of painting on ceramics is the wide range of techniques that can be used. Experiment with printing techniques such as stamping, stenciling, mono-printing, and sponging as well as drawing free-style with a brush, crayon, pen, or sgraffito tool. Motifs can be applied to plain or textured backgrounds, on their own or in combination with one another. The following techniques are covered in the individual projects, but if you want to vary them or create other designs, read the notes below.

1 Rubber stamping

You can buy ready-made rubber stamps or cut your own simple shapes. If you make your own stamps, glue the rubber motif to a wooden backing. Stamps are ideal for making repeat patterns and can be used in different colors, provided they are washed between each change of color. Small to medium stamps are good for printing on curved surfaces because they can be rolled over the surface.

2 Free-style painting

There are virtually no restrictions with free-style painting, although very straight lines or angular shapes require a certain degree of skill. Choose from the brushes described on pages 20–21 for different effects.

3 Sgraffito

With this technique, the design is scratched through the underglaze using a sgraffito tool or fine, pointed instrument to reveal the color of the bisque underneath. This will allow you to create more detailed designs than with stenciling or stamping.

4 Underglaze crayons & pencils

These are very good for outlines and for picking out details, such as a leaf and its veins.

5 Underglaze pens

These are available in different-sized nibs: thick, medium, or fine. They create harder lines than crayons or pencils, so they are good for strong outlines and bold detail. They can also be used to fill in areas with crosshatching as an alternative to even color applied with a brush.

6 Sponge stamping

Sponge stamps will give you a more open effect than rubber stamps. You can buy ready-made shapes or cut your own from high-density sponge. Sponges are more flexible than rubber stamps, so they are ideal for large, curved surfaces. Use for simple motifs only because it is difficult to cut intricately detailed designs from sponge.

7 Mono-printing

This technique, in which the motif is painted onto a paper towel, then printed onto the bisque, produces fuzzy lines that make an effective contrast with sharp ones. Mono-printing can be done on any surface because the paper towel will wrap around almost any shape or curve.

8 Stenciling

Stencils produce very crisp lines and edges. You can either buy them readymade or cut your own. Clear acetate is best. To prevent color from seeping underneath the stencil, thicken the underglaze to a paste consistency with a small amount of china clay.

1

3

6

8

Resist techniques

You can achieve some wonderful results by creating a pattern from areas that have been blocked out from the background color. This is known as the "resist" method. Resist is essentially the opposite of stenciling. For example, if you apply round stickers to a surface, paint on colored underglaze, and then remove the stickers, the resisted area forms the dot design. Resist materials can include stickers, masking tape, paper, artist's masking fluid, or wax emulsion. In general, these media are removed after applying the underglaze. If any color seeps under the resist, it can be removed with a craft knife when dry. You can also resist out more than one underglaze color by working in stages, provided that the coat of underglaze applied in a prior stage is dry before subsequent coats are applied (see 2 and 9).

Masking fluids

Masking fluids allow for great variety in the resist design, because the pattern is applied with a brush. Liquids such as latex or artist's watercolor masking fluid can be used to mask out water-based underglaze. Paint your pattern as thickly as possible, let it dry thoroughly, and then apply the underglaze. Peel away the masking fluid before firing (see 8). Wax emulsion is an alternative, but requires an additional firing to burn the wax off. It is good for spattering or for creating tiny dots, because the dots don't have to be peeled off individually (see 5 and 6).

Masking tape

Masking tape, available in different widths, is ideal for masking straight edges, bands, borders, and stripes, and works for both flat and rounded surfaces (see 3 and 7). Small pieces of tape may be cut into squares, rectangles, or triangles. Long strips tend to ripple on curved surfaces, so join shorter strips end to end.

Paper

Paper is a very successful resist medium, allowing you to mask off fairly large areas. Thin paper is ideal for wrapping around curved surfaces, while printer paper can be torn to create deckled edges (see 4). Stick paper to the surface by dampening or holding it firmly in place, then paint with underglaze while still damp. Do not let the paper become too wet or it will disintegrate.

Stickers

Self-adhesive stickers are available in many shapes and sizes, or you can cut your own from address labels (see 1, 2, 3, 9, 10, and 11).

1 One-step resist using square stickers cut from labels; handpainted dots.

2 Two-step resist using star stickers to resist out yellow and square stickers centered over stars to resist out red.

3 One-step resist using star stickers and masking tape; handpainted dots.

4 One-step resist using torn paper.

5 and 6 One-step resist using wax emulsion for painted dots.

7 One-step resist using masking tape.

8 One-step resist using masking fluid.

9 Two-step resist using small dot stickers to resist out yellow and medium dot stickers roughly placed over small dots to resist out brown; handpainted red dots.

10 One-step resist and spot glazing. Small dots were placed at random to resist out pink, then large dots were placed over the small dots to resist out glaze. All stickers were peeled off, then the resisted area of white dots was spot-glazed.

11 Two-step resist and spot glazing. Medium dot stickers were used to resist out red. Large dot stickers were centered over the resisted areas to resist out glaze for a halo effect. The stickers were peeled off, then crosses and dots were handpainted in the center of resisted areas. The area left by the first sticker was then glazed, leaving the halo unglazed.

Brushes

Brushes are available in a wide variety of shapes and sizes, from wide, flat ones to extremely fine pointed ones. Finding the most suitable brushes for you can be a learning experience. Prices vary enormously depending on the quality, so before you spend a fortune on expensive brushes, it is worth discovering which styles and techniques you prefer.

Overall, rounded-point brushes are good for detailed work and curved shapes such as petals and leaves, while flat brushes are ideal for straight lines, backgrounds, and broad areas of color. When painting outlines, you will find you have more control over brushes with shorter bristles, although longer ones will hold more underglaze.

It is a good idea to experiment with different brushes on paper first. Try varying the amount of underglaze on the brush and the pressure you apply; use different parts of the brush such as the tip or the side; vary the way you paint from slowly to quickly, and try ending the stroke by lifting the brush off abruptly or tapering off gently. You can also practice painting a continuous line in which you vary the pressure so the stroke narrows and widens.

Some of the most useful brushes for the projects in this book are shown opposite, but the four I rely on the most are a small rounded brush, a medium rounded-point brush, a fine script liner, and a 1in/2.5cm flat brush (see 3, 6, 5 and 1).

Care & cleaning

For water-based underglazes, clean your brushes with hot, soapy water when you have finished using them. If you have been applying masking fluid or wax emulsion, clean your brush immediately, according to the manufacturer's directions.

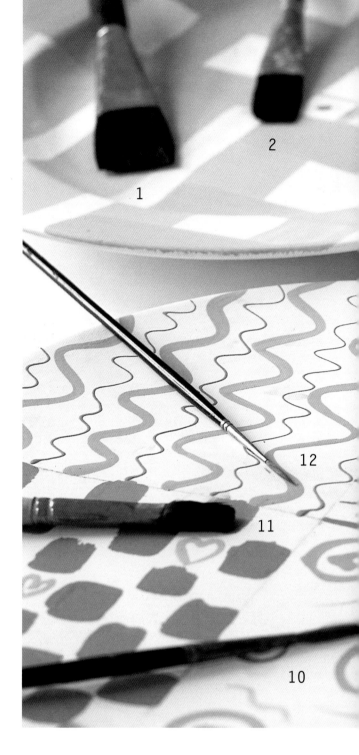

1 1in/2.5cm flat brush. Use for backgrounds and large areas of flat color as well as bold strokes, stripes, and zigzags. Squares can be made with short strokes.

2 ¾in/1.5cm flat brush. Use as for the 1in/2.5cm flat brush to create thinner stripes and smaller squares.

3 Small rounded brush. This is useful for painting dots, medium lines, and for filling in.

4 Stencil brush. This will allow you to stipple color through stencils. A small sponge can be used as an alternative.

5 **Fine script liner.** Use to paint long, continuous lines, details, and outlines.

6 **Medium rounded-point brush.** This versatile brush will allow you to paint thick and thin lines, to fill in shapes, and to create pointed shapes such as leaves by lifting the brush off at the end of each stroke.

7 **Underglaze pen.** Available in three sizes, underglaze pens are good for creating fine, even lines. They are not available as acrylic paints and so cannot be used on glazed ceramics.

8 **Underglaze pencil/crayon.** Use for adding highlights or to provide a contrast to a painted or pen line. A softer effect is produced by smudging.

9 **Fine pointed brush.** Use for small dots, fine lines, crosshatching, dashes, and outlines.

10 **Medium script liner.** This will create similar effects to the fine script liner, but with wider and larger lines.

11 **½in/1cm flat brush.** Use for stripes, squares, zigzags, and dashes. You can use stick sponges as an alternative.

12 **Extra-fine script liner.** This is a shorter, thinner version of the fine script liner and can be used for whisker-fine lines.

Planning designs

Designing is ultimately a very personal process, but there are a few considerations to help you narrow down the field of options. If you have little or no design experience, the following guidelines should help you to develop some ideas of your own.

First, consider the shape of your object. A simple plate can be treated like a circular canvas; your overall pattern will not have to accommodate extra dimensions. A container such as a pitcher or teapot will have features like a collar, handle, spout, or lid that you may want to incorporate into the design.

The object's function is another point to consider. If you are designing functional tableware, consider how it will look when in use. Do you want an elaborate, all-over design or something minimal with just a border? If you are decorating a mug, you will see the upturned base when it is lifted to the mouth or if it is hanging on a hook, so don't forget this area.

If your piece is to be used for decorative purposes only, you may already have a place for displaying it in mind, in which case the style and color you choose may be influenced by the room. If you are creating a piece as a gift, consider personalizing it with a name, design, or motif relevant to the occasion.

Positioning the design before painting

Once you have a general idea for the design, experiment on paper rather than painting straight onto the bisque. You can scale motifs up or down on a photocopier. For flat objects, you can draw a design to scale on paper. For spherical objects, stick the paper cut-out onto the object with adhesive tape. This way, you can wrap the motifs around curves and awkward shapes to get an idea of which sizes and positions look best. You can even color the motifs first to get a more complete picture of the finished piece.

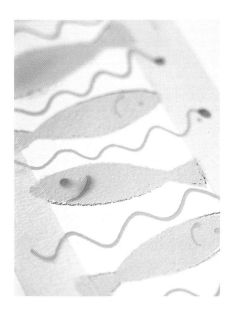

This stencil design was marked in pencil first to make a regularly spaced pattern. The pencil lines will disappear when kiln-fired.

Drawing the design in pencil

Another option is to draw your design straight onto the bisque in pencil before applying the underglaze; the graphite can be wiped off with a damp sponge if you wish to redo it, but in any event it will burn away during the firing process. Graphite does not burn off preglazed ceramics, however, so any visible marks will need to be wiped away before the object is placed in the oven.

Finding the center of a circle

Some designs require a degree of accuracy in their measurements. To find the center of a plate or round surface, draw around its circumference on a piece of paper, cut out, fold in half and half again and open up. The center point is where the folded lines cross.

Transferring motifs

Once you have decided on the position of your motifs, you will need to transfer them to the bisque. If you are not confident about drawing them freehand, and it is not possible to draw around a cardboard template, you can either transfer the motifs from tracing paper or mono-print them directly onto the surface.

Transferring paper motifs

For this method you will need tracing paper and a hard and a soft pencil. You can use the motifs at the back of the book or research other sources for inspiration. Simple designs are best to start with; enlarge or reduce them on a photocopier as necessary.

Trace the motif on tracing paper using a soft pencil. Turn the tracing over and, still using the soft pencil, scribble over the entire reverse side of the design (see 1).

Position the tracing on the bisque (scribble side down). Hold securely in place and, using a hard pencil, draw over the pencil lines, thus transferring the motif to the bisque (see 2).

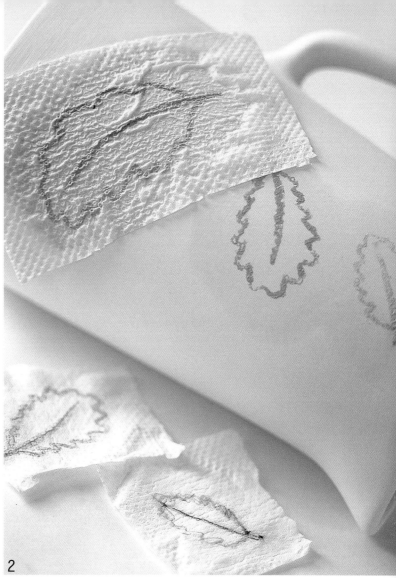

Mono-printing motifs

This wonderful technique, which gives a soft line, involves painting the motif onto a paper towel before transferring to the bisque. You are not limited to outlines, but can paint solid shapes, using more than one color. If you aren't happy with the motif you have painted, just start again, and if you make a mistake on the bisque, wipe it off with a damp sponge.

Using a soft pencil or felt pen, trace your motif onto an absorbent paper towel (thin enough to see through). Paint over the outlines with a thick coat of underglaze (see 1). Position the motif, paint side down, on the bisque, and dab it with a damp sponge several times. The paper will become transparent, and you will be able to see how much the lines are "bleeding" (see 2). (The design will be in reverse on the bisque.) When happy with the effect, peel away the paper (see 3).

If your design requires more than one motif, draw them individually on separate pieces of paper towel because you can use each one only once.

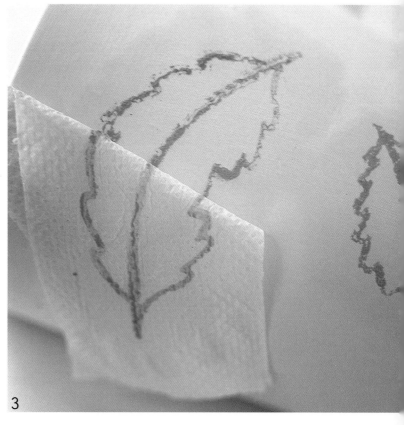

Color dynamics

Working with color presents an exciting challenge with almost limitless possibilities. When planning your design, even at the earliest stages, you need to have a vision of the effect you want to achieve; understanding the way color works will help you to turn your ideas into reality. If you want a hot, vibrant effect, this will dictate your choice of colors; conversely, muted colors tend to be more sophisticated, while some combinations of colors are cool and soothing. This is less complicated than it appears. Even if you know nothing about how color works, you don't need to do an entire course in color theory to understand some basic principles. The following are a few guidelines to help you think about some successful color combinations.

Color mixing

Most of us are familiar with the concept of primary colors; these are red, yellow, and blue, and all colors are made from a combination of them. Two primary colors mixed together produce a secondary color: orange (yellow and red); purple (red and blue); green (blue and yellow). If these colors are then mixed, tertiary colors result, for example, olive-green, turquoise-blue, and so on.

If white is added to a primary, secondary, or tertiary color, a "tint" is produced, while adding black to any color will produce a "shade". Colors are described as having the same tonal value when they have the same amount of black or white mixed into them. For example, powder-blue, pale pink and pistachio-green share the same tonal value. One way to combine colors successfully in a pattern is to work with colors of the same tone.

Complementary colors

Some combinations of colors – red and green, yellow and purple, blue and orange – seem to bring out the best in one another. Purple will appear more intense next to yellow, which in turn will appear more vivid because of its proximity to purple. If you choose combinations of complementary colors in your design, the effect will be vibrant and glowing.

Hot & cold colors

Colors can be further categorized as hot or cold, with red being the hottest color and blue the coldest. Within that range, there is a whole spectrum of colors from warm to cool – oranges and yellows being warm, and blues and greens being cool. To "warm up" blue, you could add more red, while to "cool down" orange, you could add some blue. Hot colors will dominate over cool ones, so, for example, if you create a pattern combining red and blue, the red will appear to come forward and the blue will appear to recede.

An interesting effect can be achieved by choosing a hot palette or a cold palette and then enlivening the whole with a tiny amount of the opposite. For example, in the Africa mug project (see page 38), I used hot colors but added a streak of green (cool) down some of the oval motifs. Similarly, I could have used blue and green and enlivened them with a streak of red.

How many colors to use

Designs using more than five colors can be very confusing – both to paint and to look at. Try to minimize the number of colors, but use different tones of the main color. For example, if you want a red teapot, choose two other tones of red such as orange and pink, and then contrast or highlight with a small amount of a contrasting color such as green. Another way to add interest is to mix tones of the same colors, decorating a blue and yellow mug with a darker shade of blue or yellow, for example. You could also look at working with tints and shades of one color only, such as painting a vase in purple, purple mixed with white, and purple mixed with black.

Whatever colors you choose, experiment with them on paper first. If you are using more than five colors and your design is intricate, it may help to code them with numbers on a sketch, and then refer to the sketch when painting the piece itself, as if you were painting by numbers.

Projects

I was particularly eager to work with the simplicity of this bowl and set of plates and to develop a design that complemented each piece individually, but was not too overpowering for the set as a whole. The smooth, uninterrupted curve of the deep bowl lent itself to a vertically striped pattern, which has the effect of exaggerating its height. If the bowl had been shallow, I could have created a design using horizontal lines to emphasize its width.

Heavily patterned plates can be distracting to eat from, so I lifted a detail from the bowl and applied it to each plate as an inset border only. You will notice that the border on the larger plate is much closer to the rim than on the smaller one; this is so that none of the pattern is obscured when the plates are stacked as part of the table setting.

If you want to simplify the design, use a wider brush to apply fewer, thicker stripes, and reduce the number of horizontal lines to three. Alternatively, you can replace the lines with one wide horizontal band.

The main design was worked on the bowl, with details repeated on the plates. This keeps the set from being too overwhelming when viewed together, while still creating a unifying theme.

striped noodle set

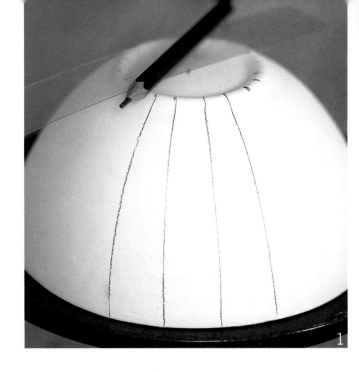

You will need

Bisque:
bowl, approximately 6in/15cm wide
large plate, approximately 11in/28cm wide
medium plate, approximately 9in/23cm wide
Acetate ruler
Pencil
Decorating wheel (optional)
Large yogurt container or similar
Masking fluid
Masking tape, 1in/2.5cm wide
Sharp knife
Utility knife (optional)
Drawing compass (optional)

Brushes

Fine script liner
1in/2.5cm flat brush
Fine pointed brush

Underglaze paints

Lilac
Dark purple

Techniques used

Painting stripes
Masking-fluid resists

Alternative designs

See pages 35-37

MARKING THE DESIGN ON THE BOWL With the bowl upturned, make a pencil mark in the center of the base; you can do this with the ruler or by eye (or see page 22). Then add marks at approximately ½in/1cm intervals around the base of the bowl. It is important that they are evenly spaced to achieve a regular striped effect. Use the ruler to align the center point with each mark around the base of the bowl. Extend it down over the side of the bowl, and draw straight lines from the base to the rim.

APPLYING THE MASKING FLUID Turn the bowl upside down on a large yogurt container or similar object so the rim is lifted clear of the work surface. Load the fine script liner with masking fluid and, using the ruler as a guide, paint over the vertical pencil lines. Clean the ruler with a cloth between each line, and make sure the masking fluid is painted on fairly thickly because this will make it easier to peel off in Step Four; it will also mean the area is properly masked out. If you make any mistakes, wait approximately 10 minutes for the fluid to dry, then peel it off and re-apply. Wash the brush in hot, soapy water as soon as you have finished.

When all the fluid is dry – it should be tacky to touch but not come off on your finger – use the flat brush to apply three separate layers of lilac underglaze over the outside of the bowl. Your brushstrokes should be vertical and painted in the same direction as the masking fluid lines or you will inadvertently peel them off. Leave to dry.

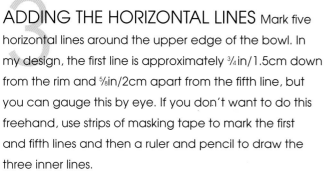

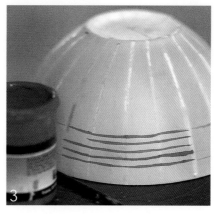

3 ADDING THE HORIZONTAL LINES Mark five
horizontal lines around the upper edge of the bowl. In
my design, the first line is approximately ¾in/1.5cm down
from the rim and ⅝in/2cm apart from the fifth line, but
you can gauge this by eye. If you don't want to do this
freehand, use strips of masking tape to mark the first
and fifth lines and then a ruler and pencil to draw the
three inner lines.

Using the fine script liner, paint the first and fifth lines
in dark purple. Load the brush fairly thickly so you don't
have to paint them more than once. Paint the lines in
sections, as shown in the photograph. In this way you
avoid constantly turning the bowl, and if a line begins
to wobble, you can straighten it up when you come to
apply the adjacent stroke. Repeat with the inner lines.

4 PEELING OFF THE MASKING FLUID Using the
tip of a sharp knife, pick up the masking-fluid lines and
peel them off with your fingers. If you painted the lines
on thickly enough, they should come away easily. If you
painted them on too thinly, however, you may find that
some of the underglaze has seeped through. If so, gently
scrape it off with a utility knife. If you used masking tape,
peel it off. The bowl is ready to glaze and fire.

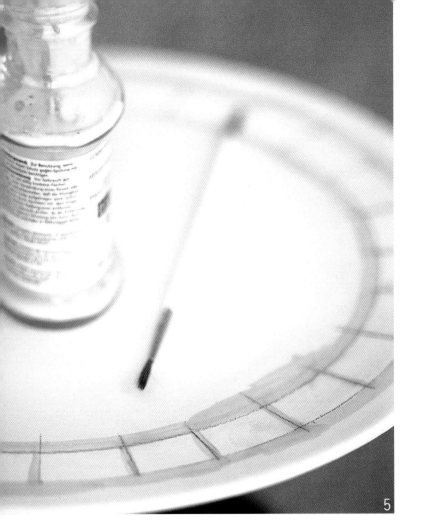

MARKING THE DESIGN ON THE PLATE

Mark the design with a pencil. The lilac band should be approximately ⅝in/2cm wide. This can be drawn free-style, or with the aid of a compass or a circular cardboard template. Draw in the crossbars at 2cm/⅝in intervals. Finally, using a fine pointed brush, paint over the lines with masking fluid, as in Step Two.

APPLYING THE UNDERGLAZE

Use the 1in/2.5cm flat brush to fill in the band with two to three layers of lilac underglaze. Let it dry, then use the fine script liner to paint the three inner lines in dark purple. Paint them in four sections at a time to avoid constantly turning the plate, and to allow you to correct the line if it starts to wobble. Leave the plate to dry, then peel away the masking fluid. The plate is now ready to glaze and fire.

For the smaller plate, repeat Steps Five and Six. The lilac band is ½in/1cm wide and set 1½in/3.5cm in from the rim; the crossbars are positioned ½in/1cm apart.

Acrylic painting

Not suitable.

Bowl & plate sets

The following illustrations are alternative designs for bowls and plates, which you can either copy or use as starting points for your own designs. These patterns suit individual pieces, as well as working well on pieces within a set.

Africa

For the bowl: first paint the bowl red, then paint green dots free-style around the rim. For the medium-sized plate: resist out a shield shape with masking fluid and paint the plate yellow. Peel off the masking fluid and add green zigzags, brown stripes, and red dots. For the large plate: paint dots around the rim in a sequence of red, orange, terracotta, yellow, brown, and green.

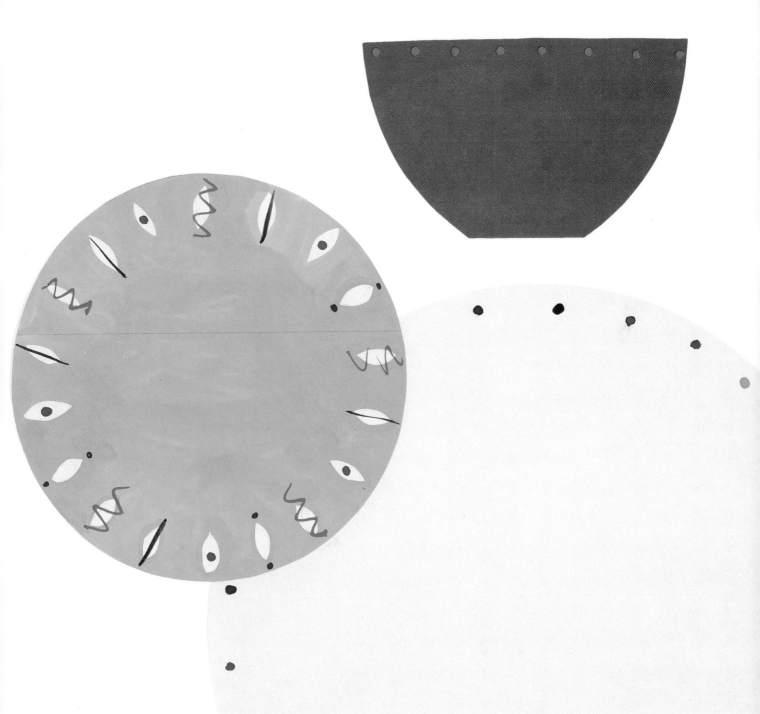

Squares

For the bowl: paint the outside of the bowl, then the square. For the small plate: resist out the squares with stickers. For the large plate: make a grid with masking tape.

Floral

For the bowl: draw two flower motifs from different angles with a graphite pencil. Paint the petals yellow, highlighting them orange and red, and paint the centers red. Fill in the background in green. Outline the petals with an underglaze pencil.
For the medium plate: draw a large, single flower in the center of the plate, then continue as for the bowl.
For the large plate: draw part of the flower motif around the edge of the plate, then continue as for the bowl.

Fish

For the bowl: paint the turquoise wiggly line.
Draw evenly spaced fish and sgraffito them.
Paint the fish eyes red. For the large plate:
paint two wiggly lines, and continue as for
the bowl, adding sgraffito wavy lines. Paint
the eyes. For the medium plate: paint the
plate turquoise. Draw the fish, then sgraffito
them and the wavy lines. Paint the eyes.

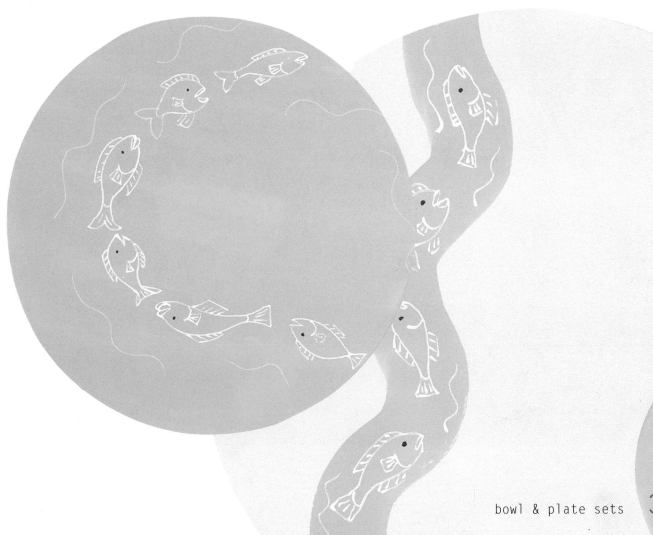

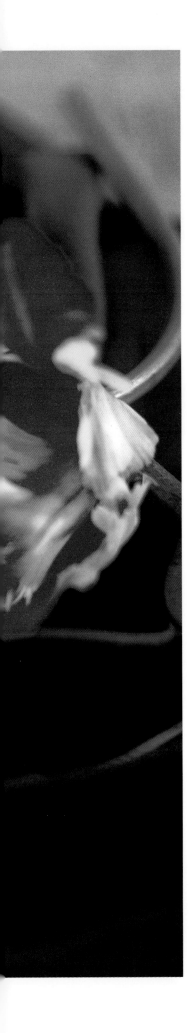

The design for this mug evokes

the rich colors of Africa and the dramatic shape of a Zulu warrior's shield. It is based on an informal repeat pattern which I color-coded on the mug before I began. Although this mug has straight sides, the pattern will also suit one with rounded sides.

I chose a strong orange-red for the background color and left a white halo around each shield so they would stand out. I picked a strong green for the final touches – the zigzags and stripes on some of the shields and the zigzag on the handle. The four colors used for the shields are equally vivid, but the yellow was applied in one coat rather than three. The result – a less saturated color – adds variety and enlivens the design.

If you want to create a set, this design can be transferred to a pitcher, or you might like to choose just two of the colors and simply paint one color overall and the second color on the rim.

The uneven haloes around the shields on this mug help to enliven the overall design. The bottom of the mug has been painted to continue the design, adding extra interest.

Africa mug

You will need

Bisque mug
Pencil
Decorating wheel (optional)
Thin cardboard for template
Utility knife or scissors

Brushes

Medium rounded-point brush
1in/2.5cm flat brush
Fine script liner

Underglaze paints

Brown
Tan
Egg-yolk yellow
Orange-red
Dark green
Deep red

Techniques used

Handpainting
Transferring your design

Alternative designs

See pages 42-43

DRAWING ON THE DESIGN
Draw the shield motifs on to the mug with a pencil (either free-style or using the template on page 83). Position three shields at regular intervals close to the top, and three more directly beneath them at the bottom. Allow the design to "fall off" at either the top or the bottom, so you have a complete shield and a portion of a shield in each pair. Finally, center a single shield between each pair, and add one to the base of the mug. When positioning the shields around the mug, you do not need to be precise, but if you want a more formal-looking result, you can measure the spaces between them.

FILLING IN THE PATTERN WITH COLOR
Assign a number to each of the four colors you have chosen for the shields and key them into the design randomly before you begin painting. Make sure neighboring shields aren't painted the same color. Using the medium rounded-point brush, color each shield accordingly. A single layer of paint will look watery when fired, so apply three layers for an opaque finish. Here, egg-yolk yellow paint was applied in a single layer to add variety to the design. Paint a shield on the base.

FILLING IN THE BACKGROUND Using the medium rounded-point brush, fill in the background, painting three layers of underglaze roughly around the shields to leave a halo around each one. Paint the rim of the mug with two layers of the same color. Hold the brush horizontally, using the middle of it, not the tip, to apply the paint. Don't worry if any paint accidentally drips inside the mug; all you need to do is wipe it away with a damp sponge.

ADDING THE ZIGZAGS The zigzag pattern is added in a free, spontaneous way. Using a fine script liner, quickly paint a zigzag pattern down some of the shields. Start at the top and paint five zigzag strokes downward. If you are apprehensive about painting straight onto the shield, practice this movement beforehand on paper. The key is to relax and not worry about being too precise. For interest, finish by painting on dots and a zigzag or stripe down the center of the handle. To add variety, leave some shields plain and decorate others with a stripe in the center. Leave to dry. The mug is now ready for glazing and firing.

Acrylic painting

Make sure the base colors are dry before adding the zigzags, stripes, and dots or the colors will merge. Do not paint the rim or the inside of the mug.

See also page 13.

Tea & coffee mugs

Mugs are fun to decorate. You can be as daring as you like with your design because you don't have to take other factors such as the appearance of food into consideration, as you would with a bowl or plate. Don't forget to decorate the base of the mug, and you can always paint the inside, too.

1 Use masking fluid to create a free-style resist, then apply a pale blue wash. Lightly load a dry brush to create a streaked effect in dark blue.

2 Apply gray wash as a background. Paint, stamp, or stencil six-pointed stars with a circle inside. Fill in the centers of the stars and add dots.

3 Paint thick yellow lines followed by orange, overlapping colors to create different shades. Use a thinner brush to add red lines and dots.

4 Put masking tape around the base. Paint a shield, then the background, leaving a halo. Remove the tape. Paint the base and handle. Add dots and a zigzag.

5 Trace or draw the motif from page 82. Paint the bird, then the pale leaves, dark leaves, and handle. Add the lines with underglaze crayon or pencil.

6 Resist out the flowers with fluid. Paint the mug. Remove the fluid. Paint the red centers, taupe outlines, and handle. Crayon the blue lines and dots.

7 Trace the fish motif from page 86. Paint the gills and tail lines with a blue wash. Use a fine brush for the remaining details.

8 Paint the mug pink. Apply strips of masking tape. Add star stickers. Paint taupe. Remove all the resists. Paint the lilac dots and rim.

9 Paint the mug yellow. Then paint dark bands around the top and bottom of the mug. Paint the dogs. Sgraffito the white lines.

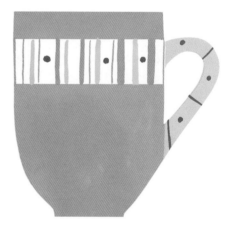

10 Paint the cup pale yellow. With a fine brush, paint a mix of small and large letters in lilac and brown. If you prefer, stencil the letters.

11 Use masking tape as a resist for the band at the top of the mug. Paint the background, peel off the tape, then paint the lines and dots free-style.

A teapot is one of the more challenging objects to decorate because the lid, knob, handle, and spout all need to be accommodated within the design. Intricate patterns can be difficult to wrap around these areas, unless you are using a free-style technique. My solution was to paint a pale wash all over the teapot, and then stencil and stamp a random pattern of flowers on top. This way, I could avoid awkward curves and grooves but still incorporate the handle, spout, and lid into the design by stenciling a few flower heads on them. You can adapt the technique by using the stencil instead of the stamp for the stem and leaves. For a more painterly effect, apply all the motifs free-style.

Carry elements of the pattern onto a set of cups and saucers – you might want to repeat the flower heads minus the leaves and stalks on the cups, and color-wash the saucers to match the teapot.

The spontaneity and freshness of this floral pattern are partly a result of practical concerns: randomly spaced motifs are easier to apply to irregular shapes than formal repeat patterns.

Floral teapot

You will need

Large bisque teapot
Flower-head, stem, and leaf motifs
from page 82
Pencil
Small sponge
Marker pen
Clear acetate for the stencil
Cutting mat
Utility knives, including one with a
rotating blade, or small, sharp scissors
Sheet of rubber, ½in/1cm thick,
for the stamp
Wooden block for the stamp
Adhesive for the wood and rubber

Brushes

1-2in/2.5-5cm flat brush
Small rounded brush
Stencil brush (optional)

Underglaze paints

Lemon yellow
Egg-yolk yellow
Red-orange
Dark blue
Turquoise stamp pad
China clay to thicken the underglaze
for stenciling

Techniques used

Applying a wash
Stenciling and stamping

Alternative designs

See pages 49-51

APPLYING A WASH Dilute an ounce of lemon-yellow underglaze with two ounces of water to make the wash. Using the flat brush, paint the teapot, including the rim, handle, and the outside of the lid, with a single coat.

MARKING THE DESIGN With a pencil, mark crosses for the positions of the flower heads. This design includes nine on each side, plus one on the handle, one on the spout, and five on the lid. Allow space for stems below a few of the flower heads. Next, using a clean, damp sponge, dab off the areas of wash where the flowers will be, creating a halo effect.

MAKING THE STENCIL
Using a marker pen, trace the two flower-head templates from page 82 on a sheet of acetate. Leave an area of clear acetate around the motifs to act as a paint guard when you stencil on the color. Place the acetate on a cutting mat and use a utility knife with a rotating blade to cut out the flower-head templates (the rotating blade will help you to cut out curved lines). Hold the acetate firmly on the cutting mat and be very careful as you cut. Alternatively, you can cut out the stencils with a pair of small, sharp scissors, starting in the center of the stencil and cutting out the motif only, leaving the surrounding area intact.

MAKING THE STAMP
Trace the stem and leaf motif from page 82 on the sheet of rubber. Using a utility knife with a stationary blade, cut out the motif carefully. You will find you cannot cut through the rubber in one try, so cut a shallow outline of the motif first and go back to cut around it a second time. Glue the stamp to a block of wood and let it dry.

5

APPLYING THE STENCIL COLOR

For successful stenciling, the lemon-yellow and the egg-yolk yellow underglazes need to have a paste consistency, so thicken a teaspoon of each with a small amount of china clay. Using your pencil marks as a positional guide, stencil the lemon-yellow, star-shaped flowers, followed by the egg-yolk yellow rounded flowers. To do this, dip the sponge into the underglaze and squeeze off any excess. Holding the acetate in position, gently dab on the paint with the sponge. If you prefer, use a stencil brush instead of a sponge. It may help to practice stenciling on a spare piece of bisque first.

Next, press the rubber stamp on the turquoise stamp pad, and stamp stems and leaves underneath a few of the star-shaped flowers. You may want to practice this beforehand, too, on a spare piece of bisque. As the teapot has a curved edge, it is best to apply the print by carefully rolling the stamp from top to bottom, to maintain even coverage. Leave it to dry.

ADDING THE DETAIL
Paint the knob with two or three coats of lemon yellow. Use the small rounded brush to add red-orange dots and swirls to the lemon-yellow flowers, and dark blue dots to the egg-yolk yellow flowers. Let it dry. The teapot is now ready to glaze and fire.

Acrylic painting

If the acrylic is too thin, leave a small amount on a saucer for 10–20 minutes to thicken.

See also page 13.

Variation

Instead of stamping, stencil or paint the stems and leaves free-style. If you are stenciling, thicken the underglaze with china clay as in Step Five.

6

Teapots

Free-style painting and resist designs are particularly suited to the irregular shape of a teapot. The following alternative designs will give you a few ideas and, hopefully, encourage you to experiment.

Chinese
Trace the Chinese calligraphy motifs from page 92 onto the teapot body and lid, and paint over them with masking fluid. Paint the knob, the tip of the spout, and a line down the handle with masking fluid. Paint the teapot with a blue wash, then spatter it darker blue.

Spotted
Place large stickers on the teapot body, and smaller ones on the handle and lid. Paint a taupe wash over the entire teapot. With a dry stiff brush, drag a full-strength color over the teapot for a streaky effect. Paint full-strength color on the handle, knob, lip, and edge of the spout.

Africa
Draw the shields. Paint the background and shields, leaving haloes around them. Paint the lines, zigzags and dots, the handle, and collar.

Rounded vases

Ornamental vases can be decorated much more
exuberantly than those used for flowers; paint them in
softer colors so as not to clash with the blooms.

Green leaves
Cut a sponge into a leaf shape. Press it into
green paint and stamp it randomly on the vase.
Paint the outlines and stems olive green.

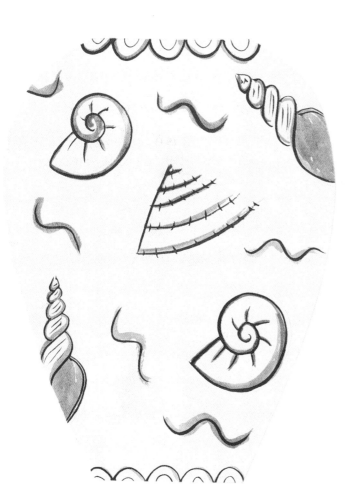

Seashells
Transfer the shell motifs on page 87 on the
vase and paint them with a blue wash. Paint
the dark blue areas with a fine liner.

Ovals on striped panel
Apply tape to create two straight lines. Paint
three layers of taupe. Sgraffito white ovals
and use underglaze pen for the brown ovals.

Oranges & lemons

Apply masking tape to the vase to mark a
straight line. Outline the lemons with masking
fluid. Paint the vase orange. Paint the
oranges, or use underglaze crayon or pen.

Spotted

Place star stickers over the pitcher and paint
it orange. Place round stickers over the stars.
Paint the pitcher green. Paint on the dots.

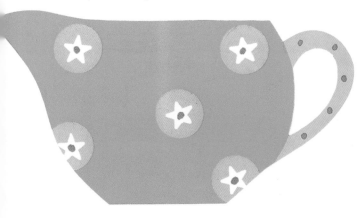

Rounded pitchers

When designing patterns for pitchers, remember to
incorporate the lip and the handle into your design.
You may want to extend the body pattern to the handle,
as with the fish design, or treat it differently, as with the
apples. You could link your pattern to the use of the item,
say a cow on a milk pitcher or herbs on a gravy boat.

Apples

Paint an outline of the apples and leaves, as
well as the stalks and veins, in masking fluid.
Paint the apples and leaves, making sure you
paint over the masking-fluid outline. Paint the
handle in stripes.

Fish

Paint wide stripes of yellow and pink down the
pitcher. Transfer a fish motif (see page 86) on
to the yellow stripes. Paint the fish and the
dots deep pink.

Because one of the features

of this plate is its rim, the obvious approach would have been to use it as the main focus of decoration. Instead, I chose to create a more unusual effect by running a band of decoration right through the center of the plate, using a simple pattern that would not compete with or distract from any food. If your plate is for display purposes only, you might want to consider a more elaborate design (see pages 56–57).

I created a straight-edged panel of decoration by extending the pattern over the edges of the masking-tape resist. This way, the fish were squared off at each end when the tape was removed.

Experiment with other designs, perhaps building a pattern around a fruit or vegetable theme, using motifs such as oranges, lemons, tomatoes, or peas in a pod.

If you don't want to use the complementary colors of orange and blue, then try the other combinations of green and red, or yellow and purple.

Fish plate

You will need

Bisque dinner plate, approximately
11in/28cm wide (rim optional)
Pencil
Acetate ruler
Masking tape, 1in/2.5cm wide
Marker pen
Fish motif from page 83
Clear acetate for the stencil
Cutting mat
Rotary cutter or small sharp scissors
Small sponge

Brush

Stencil brush (optional)

Underglaze paints

Egg-yellow yolk
Turquoise
Medium blue underglaze pen
China clay to thicken the underglaze
for stenciling

Techniques used

Stenciling
Using underglaze pens

Alternative designs

See pages 56-57

CUTTING OUT THE STENCIL Before creating the stencil, you will need to mark a 2in-/5cm-wide panel on the plate with masking tape. To do this, draw a line through the center of the plate, then mark the rim 1in/2.5cm away on each side of the central line. Use these points as a guide for positioning the strips of masking tape.

Using a marker pen, trace the fish motif from page 83 on a sheet of acetate. Leave an area of clear acetate around the motif to act as a paint guard when you stencil on the color. Next, place the acetate on a cutting mat and use a rotary cutter to cut out the fish motif (this will help you to cut around the curved lines). Hold the acetate firmly and cut carefully. Alternatively, cut out the stencil with a small pair of scissors, starting in the center and cutting out the motif shape only so that the surrounding area is left intact.

APPLYING THE COLOR

Before stenciling, it is best to mark the position of the motifs. Place one fish in the middle of the panel and then one at each end. Fill in with six evenly spaced fish, placing them head to tail. Check that the noses and tails fall fractionally onto the tape itself, so they will be squared off when you remove the tape. Judge the spacing by eye, and if your plate is a different size to the one used here, adjust the number of fish and the spacing accordingly.

In order to stencil, your underglaze will need to have a paste consistency, so thicken both colors with a small amount of china clay. Stencil the fish in alternate colors of egg-yolk yellow and turquoise. To do this, dip the sponge into the underglaze and squeeze off any excess. Hold the acetate in position and gently dab on the color with the sponge. If you prefer, a stencil brush may be used instead of the sponge. It may help to practice stenciling on a spare piece of bisque first.

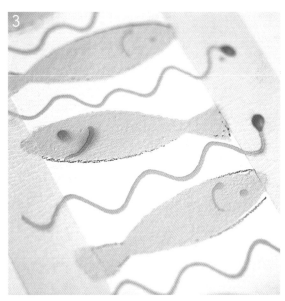

ADDING THE DECORATION

Use the blue underglaze pen to draw the decorative lines between the fish. Draw them in one continuous movement, beginning and ending on the tape, so that any blobs will not appear on the plate. Still using the underglaze pen, add the fin and eye detail. Leave to dry, then remove the tape. The plate is now ready for glazing and firing.

Acrylic painting

Paint the squiggly lines and details with a fine brush.
See also page 13.

Plates & platters

Plates and platters are easy to decorate because
of their flat surfaces, and almost any type of design
can be tried. You can make use of the rims by working
them into your design with a border pattern.

Numbers

Cut out different-sized numbers from paper.
Dampen them and press them onto the rim. Paint
a thin band of masking fluid on the inside rim,
and paint the rim blue.

Abstract

Using brushes of various sizes, paint thick,
thin, and wiggly lines over the entire plate.

Swirls

Paint the yellow outer band and terracotta
circle, followed by the orange band. With a
fine script liner, paint the flower outline and
the purple and red dashes.

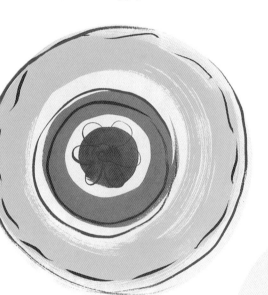

Floral

Place two strips of masking
tape across the plate
to create a central band
for decorating. Stencil,
stamp, or paint the flowers,
leaves, and stalks. Paint
the highlights with a fine
pointed brush or an
underglaze pen.

Africa

Resist out the shields with masking fluid. Paint
the rim. Remove the fluid. Paint the shields,
leaving a halo. Paint on the lines and zigzags.

Leaf

Paint the rim of the plate. Stencil the leaf. Sgraffito lines on the leaves and rim.

Face

Resist out the dots with masking fluid. Paint the rim. Peel off the fluid and fill in the dots, leaving a halo. Paint the face.

Shoe

Paint a yellow band around the rim. Paint orange stripes at intervals on top, then thin purple lines and dots. Mono-print the shoe.

Fish

Resist out the fish shape with masking fluid. Colorwash the sea, peel off the fluid, then paint the fish, starting with the light colors.

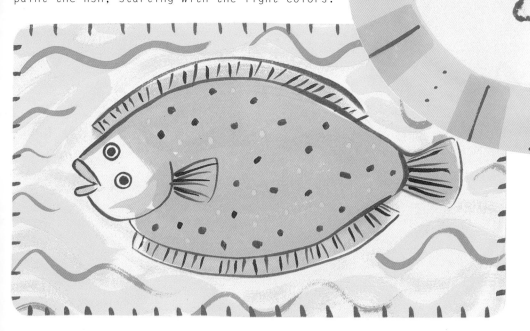

You can create some very interesting effects with flat and glossy finishes by leaving some parts of your bisque unglazed. A cup and saucer are ideal for this because you can treat the two pieces in subtly different ways. As an unglazed surface is slightly rough to the touch, glaze the top part of the cup so it is more comfortable to drink from. Equally, you should glaze the saucer because spilled coffee and tea may stain a matte surface.

For this cup and saucer, I created an abstract design, based on children's candy, using stickers to resist out rectangular shapes and colors that were complementary to the design. Of course, you can also choose more figurative designs for the two pieces, allowing you to link them thematically. For example, you might paint a lemon on the cup and a slice of lemon on the saucer, or team a cup decorated with a vivid red tomato with a bright green saucer.

The success of this design is due in part to the combination of flat and glossy textures with a subtle color palette. Repeat the pattern, varying the color relationships, to create a set that is linked but not identical.

candy cup & saucer

You will need

Bisque:
cup, approximately 5in/12cm wide
saucer, approximately 8in/20cm wide
Acetate ruler
Pencil
Masking tape, 1in/2.5cm wide
Rectangular stickers, measuring
approximately ¾ x 1in/2 x 2.5cm
Utility knife (optional)
Sharp knife
Small sponge

Brushes

Flat 1in/2.5cm brush
Small rounded brush

Underglaze paints

Deep pink
Underglaze pen or pencil (optional)
Lavender
Pale yellow
Taupe
Clear glaze
China clay to thicken the underglaze
if necessary

Techniques used

Sticker resist
Using flat-finish underglaze

Alternative designs

See pages 62-63

APPLYING THE STICKERS With a pencil or a strip of masking tape, mark a line all the way around the cup, ⅜in/8mm from the rim. Apply the stickers at even intervals around the cup, aligning their tops just below the masking tape or pencil line. The stickers must not overlap the tape. it is best to start opposite the handle and then to work your way back toward it. This cup used 16 stickers spaced at ¼in/5mm intervals. If your cup is a different shape or size, you may need to adapt the number and spacing of the stickers accordingly. Remove the masking tape if used.

APPLYING THE BACKGROUND COLOR

Make sure the stickers are firmly in place, especially around the edges. Test the thickness of the underglaze on the bottom of your cup. If it is very thin, it could seep under the stickers, so you may need to thicken it slightly with china clay. If you want to sign the cup, resist out an area on the underside by placing a sticker in the center before painting.

When you are confident of the thickness of the underglaze, use the flat brush to apply two to three coats of deep pink to the cup, including the underside. Extend the underglaze up to the top of the rim, but exclude the handle. Leave to dry. Remove the stickers by easing them up with the tip of a knife and then peeling them away. If any of the underglaze has crept under the stickers, simply scrape it off with a utility knife.

If you are signing your cup, peel off the sticker from the bottom, then write your signature on the unpainted area with an underglaze pen or pencil. Paint the saucer with two to three coats of deep pink and leave to dry.

ADDING THE DETAIL

Using a small rounded brush, fill in the resist rectangles with three coats of underglaze to achieve a dense color. I used lavender, pale yellow, and taupe in a random order, and left a few rectangles uncolored. Some were decorated with free-style dots in the same color scheme. Paint the handle with three coats of taupe underglaze. If any of the underglaze has dripped into the inside of the rim, wipe it off with a damp sponge. Leave to dry.

Acrylic painting

A similar effect can be achieved with acrylic paint by painting the lower half of the cup paler pink.

4

APPLYING THE CLEAR GLAZE

To achieve a flat finish around the lower half of the cup, you will need to mask it out to protect it from the glaze. Make sure the cup is completely dry, then wrap a strip of masking tape around it just ⅜ in/8mm below the colored rectangles. Glaze the top section of the cup and handle using the flat brush. Don't worry that the glaze appears an opaque white; it will become transparent in the firing process. Glaze the saucer and underside of the cup. Remove the masking tape from the cup. The cup and saucer are now ready for firing.

Cups & saucers

Think about the relationship of the cup to the saucer; they should relate to each other in some way, such as color, motif, or theme. If the cups are large, you could decorate the insides. Don't forget the handle.

Tulips

Paint the cup pink. Stencil tulips on the cup and the unpainted saucer. Paint the stems and dots.

Spots

Place small round stickers in rows on the cup, then paint the cup yellow and the handle brown. For the saucer, use larger stickers and place them evenly around the rim.

Stripy

Place tape one-third of the way down the cup to make a straight line. Paint the cup and saucer. Peel off the tape. Sgraffito the lines.

Abstract

Paint a blue wash over the cup and saucer. Draw on your design, then paint it the same shade of blue, but using the paint undiluted.

Leaf

Cut a sponge into a leaf shape and cut out the veins. Stamp on the design. Paint a green band around the saucer. On the cup, paint a red stripe on the handle and a green rim.

Floral

Stencil, stamp, or paint the flowers and leaves. Add the highlights, swirls, and dots. Paint the handle pale green with a dark green stripe. Paint the rims the same dark green.

Chicken

Paint the center of the saucer and the cup orange. Transfer the chicken from page 89 to the cup. Use purple underglaze pen or paint for the chicken, likewise the handle, rim, and squiggle. Paint red scallops inside the cup.

Africa

Paint shields around the top of the cup, then paint all of the inside. Paint the saucer and handle the same color red. Add green lines, zigzags and dots, and a stripe on the handle.

When decorating a bowl, one of your first decisions will be whether to focus on the inside or outside as the main area of interest. Of course, you could decorate both, but that can be overpowering; limiting the pattern to one side will have a greater impact. As this bowl was fairly deep, I chose to focus on the exterior so the inside would not compete with the food, although I echoed the design on the inside with a single mono-printed mint leaf.

If your bowl is shallow, it may make more sense to decorate the inside because it will be seen more clearly. Designs for plates can be adapted easily to suit shallow bowls, so refer also to pages 35–37 and 56–57.

Since this is a salad bowl, I decided to complement its function by decorating it with motifs of mint, sage, basil, and bay leaves. I printed one of each design in alternating panels, and then chose two lighter shades of green for the remaining panels.

You could experiment with this basic idea, perhaps repeating one leaf only.

This design developed through considering the bowl's form and function. Because the bowl is fairly deep, it made sense to concentrate the design on the outside.

leafy bowl

You will need

Deep bisque bowl, approximately 9in/23cm
diameter and 3¹/₂in/9cm high
Large yogurt container or similar
Felt pen
Acetate ruler
Masking tape, 1in/2.5cm wide
Utility knife (optional)
Leaf motifs from page 83
Paper towel
Small sponge

Brushes

1in/2.5cm flat brush
Fine pointed brush

Underglaze paints

Mint green
Sage green
Olive green
Underglaze crayon or pencil (optional)

Techniques used

Mono-printing (see also page 25)

Alternative designs

See pages 68-69

1

MARKING THE DESIGN With the bowl upturned, mark the center of the base with a pencil; you can do this by eye. or see page 22. Mark eight equal sections, as if you were dividing a cake into segments. Take a long strip of masking tape and align its left edge with one of the pencil lines on the base, then stick it down from the center of the base to the rim. Make sure it is properly stuck down, running flat over the curves and wrapping firmly under the rim. Align the right edge of a second strip of masking tape with the next pencil line, to the right of your first strip, and stick it down. Repeat this process by sticking strips of tape down in the alternate triangle sections. You now have eight unmasked panels around the side of the bowl: four wide ones, which will be painted, alternating with four narrower ones, which will be left unpainted.

MONO-PRINTING THE LEAVES Use a felt pen
to trace the four leaf motifs on separate paper towels.
On the reverse of each paper towel, following the felt-
pen lines, outline the motifs in a thick coat of olive-green
underglaze using the fine pointed brush.

Position the first leaf in the center of one of the
blank panels, with the painted side facing the
bisque. (If you are doing this with the bowl upside down,
make sure your image is also upside down.) Dampen a
small sponge with water and dab it onto the paper towel
until you see the paint bleeding through. Continue
dabbing until you have achieved the desired effect,
then remove the towel. Repeat by printing the three
other leaves in the remaining blank panels.

At this stage you could mono-print the inside of
the bowl with a small leaf or add your signature to the
underside with underglaze crayon or pen. The bowl is
now ready to glaze and fire.

APPLYING THE COLOR Turn the bowl upside
down on a large yogurt container or similar object so the
rim is lifted off the work surface. This will make it easier to
paint. Identify the four wide panels to be painted (these
alternate with four narrow ones). Using the flat brush,
apply three coats of mint-green underglaze to the two
alternate wide panels. Clean the brush and apply three
coats of sage green to the two remaining wide panels.
Leave to dry before carefully peeling away the masking
tape. If any paint has seeped under the tape, scrape it
off with a utility knife.

Acrylic painting

Be careful not to wet the sponge
in Step Three too much.
See also page 13.

Deep bowls

Whether they are to be used for food or are just ornamental, deep bowls lend themselves to being painted on the inside as well as the outside. The design on the outside of a high-sided bowl can be mirrored on the inside with a small motif, or the inside can simply be painted in a contrasting color. Shallow bowls can be treated in much the same way as plates because they provide a large, uninterrupted surface for decoration.

1 Paint or stencil the fruit and leaves. Paint the background, leaving haloes around the fruit and leaves. Use a fine brush or pen for the outlines.

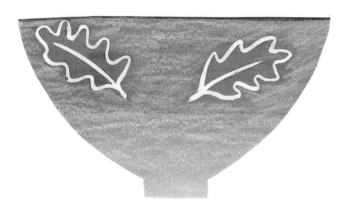

2 Use masking fluid or wax resist to paint the leaves. Then paint two bands of color. Use crayon or pencil over the bands. Remove the masking fluid.

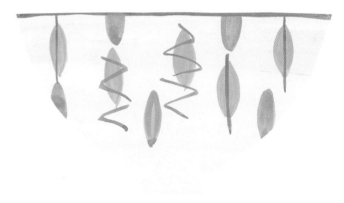

3 Paint or stencil the shields. Paint the background, then add the zigzags, vertical lines, and the brown rim.

4 Paint the apples red, followed by the orange, then white highlights. Paint the leaves. Draw on loose outlines with underglaze crayon or pencil.

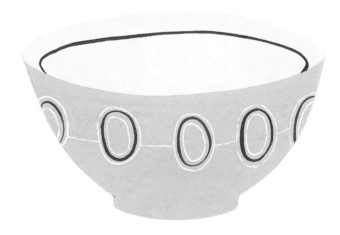

5 Paint the outside of the bowl. Sgraffito the white ovals and linking lines. Add the brown ovals and inside band with underglaze pen or paint.

6 Paint the flowers and leaves free-style. Fill in the background with bold brush strokes. Add the details with an underglaze pencil.

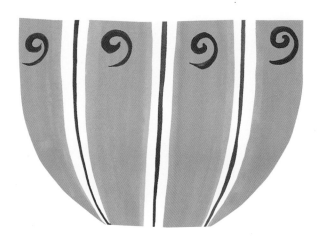

7 Paint tapering pale blue stripes down the bowl. Add the scrolls and thin vertical lines between the stripes in dark blue.

8 Paint bold bands of graduated color free-style around the bowl, starting with the ocher at the top and finishing with crimson at the bottom.

9 Paint the bowl with a thin layer of purple. Leave to dry and then sgraffito a herringbone pattern just below the rim of the bowl.

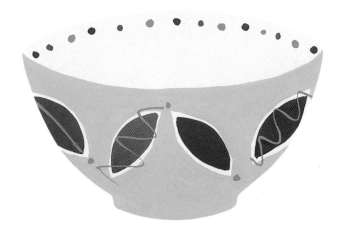

10 Paint the shields, followed by the background, leaving haloes around the shields. Add the zigzags, stripes, and dots.

11 Paint the peas using light green first and finishing with dark green. Paint the inside yellow and streak it green with a sponge or brush.

deep bowls 69

When you plan a design for a pitcher, you need to consider how to treat the lip. If it is large enough, you can extend the pattern over it. I chose a simple yet strong design of a bird within a square because it complements the clean, unfussy lines of the piece. The lines of sgraffito will show up more clearly if they are scratched into a dark background to reveal the pale clay body underneath. I used French blue, but the choice of colors is up to you. To incorporate the rest of the pitcher into the design, I continued the French blue in a stripe down the handle, and added turquoise to the rim.

Individual elements of the motif can be used to create more complex patterns. For example, lift a single leaf from the motif, set it within a square, and then use it as a repeating pattern, alternating with a single bird. This is just one of the many possibilities; you can develop countless others.

The clean simplicity of the pitcher design is enhanced by the graphic style of the bird motif. The bird's beak is a witty echo of the pitcher's lip.

Bird pitcher

You will need

Bisque pitcher
Decorating wheel (optional)
Bird motif from page 82 (it is important
to have this ready before you paint)
Sgraffito tool
Utility knife (optional)

Brushes

2in/5cm flat brush
³/₄in/1.5cm flat brush

Underglaze paints

French blue
Turquoise

Techniques

Tracing and transferring motifs
Sgraffito

Alternative designs

See pages 74-75

1

APPLYING THE PAINT Draw a 2in/5cm square in pencil on the pitcher as a guide for the area to be painted. Try to position it approximately two-thirds of the way up and centered between lip and handle. I drew mine free-style; the pencil burns off in the firing process, so it doesn't matter if you make a mistake and need to draw over it. Alternatively, you could trace it, measure it on the pitcher with a ruler, or even draw around a square template. Load the 2in/5cm flat brush with French blue underglaze and fill in the square by painting a single stroke from left to right. Try to do this in one thick coat only, lifting the brush off the pitcher at the end of the square so you can see the effect of the bristles. If the underglaze splatters slightly, it can be washed off or left to create a spontaneous, freehand effect. Leave the paint until it begins to dry and the color starts to lighten. This can take as little as one minute, but drying times vary depending on the bisque and the room temperature.

2 SGRAFFITO THE BIRD MOTIF

Transfer the bird motif to the pitcher using the prepared tracing. The underglaze may still be a little damp, but the tracing paper will not stick. Scratch through the lines with the sgraffito tool, beginning with the square, then the bird, and finally the leaves. If the incised lines begin to leave a bur, the underglaze is not quite dry enough. In this case, leave it a little longer and remove the bur with a utility knife before glazing.

3 PAINTING THE HANDLE AND RIM

Load the ¾in/1.5cm flat brush with French blue underglaze and paint a stripe down the handle, working as swiftly as you can from top to bottom and extending the color as far out to the edge as possible. Relax as you paint to create a fluid brushstroke. To give a little more control while painting the rim, place the pitcher on a decorating wheel. Still using the ¾in/1.5cm flat brush, paint the rim with two layers of turquoise underglaze. It is important to stroke the paint onto the rim using the middle rather than the tip of the brush. Hold the brush horizontally.

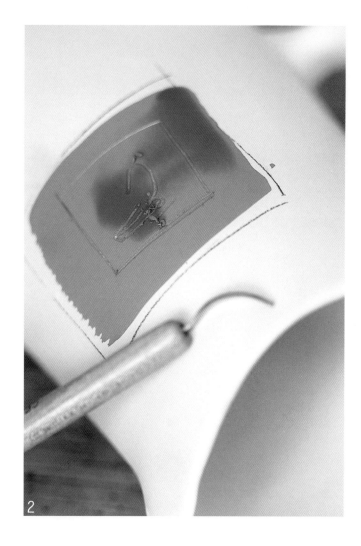

2

3

4 PAINTING THE OTHER SIDE

To repeat the motif on the other side, reverse the tracing so the bird's beak is facing out toward the lip of the pitcher.

Acrylic painting

Tracing paper may stick to damp acrylic, so you will need to let the paint dry before beginning Step Two. You can sgraffito directly onto wet acrylic if you are drawing your motif free-style.

See also page 13.

Vases & pitchers

The tapering shape of a vase can limit the type of decoration you choose. Vertical stripes, for example, are probably best avoided because it is difficult to make them taper as the vase narrows. Horizontal stripes are much easier to work with. If your vase has a lip, try to incorporate it into your design. If that's not possible, disguise it with an all-over pattern.

1 Colorwash the vase yellow. Apply strips of tape. Paint the unmasked sections full-strength yellow. Stencil the flowers. Paint their centers.

2 Apply tape one-fifth of the way down the vase to make a straight line. Add star stickers. Paint the band. Remove the stickers and tape. Paint the dots.

3 Paint or stencil the shield. Then paint the rim of the vase, followed by the zigzags, vertical lines, and dots.

4 & 5 left: Paint the vase purple. Use tape for the bands and fluid for the details. Paint mid- then dark purple. right: Use tape and fluid. Paint the stripes.

6 Trace a bird motif from page 89, then paint, starting with the pale colors. Outline the design with paint or underglaze pen or pencil.

7 & 8 Paint the color bands. Add the pattern with underglaze pen. right: Make a straight line with tape. Paint the lower section. Dab on the spots.

9 Colorwash the pitcher. Wipe off some paint with a damp sponge. Stencil the fish. Sgraffito the white lines and use underglaze pen for the dark lines.

I prefer to use very simple designs on small objects; elaborate patterns can appear too fussy on a small piece. With salt and pepper shakers, I start by considering how to treat the holes. They should not interrupt the design, so you can either avoid them altogether, as I have here by drawing stripes on each side of them, or make them part of the design. For example, you could incorporate them into a pattern of flower heads, making the holes the center of the flowers.

I varied the design by echoing the stripes on the pepper shaker around just the base of the salt shaker. A speckled glaze on the salt shaker creates interest and complements the colored stripes of the pepper shaker. This approach would work equally well for other objects such as egg cups (see pages 80–81 for alternative designs).

Small objects do not require ornate patterns; well-chosen colors and a simple decorative device will often be enough. The crayon lines are deliberately spontaneous in feel, making an effective contrast with the minimalist design of the shakers.

salt & pepper shakers

You will need

Bisque salt and pepper shakers
Masking tape, 1in/2.5 cm wide
Pencil
Acetate ruler (optional)
Fine knitting needle or similar

Brush

1in/2.5cm flat brush

Underglaze

Green speckled glaze
Underglaze crayons or pencils in
six colors (lime green, sage green,
bottle green, gray, royal blue,
and lilac were used here)
Clear glaze

Techniques used

Using underglaze crayons or pencils
Applying clear glaze

Alternative designs

See pages 80-81

1 MARKING THE DESIGN

Draw pencil lines down the pepper shaker, and around the base of the salt shaker, as guides for the colored stripes. They can be evenly spaced, but I prefer a more irregular effect. It doesn't matter if the lines are wobbly. If you prefer, you can use the ruler as a guide. Wrap masking tape around the bottom of the salt pot, ½in/1cm up from the base.

2 APPLYING THE SPECKLE GLAZE

Paint three coats of speckled glaze over the salt shaker. (If it dribbles in to the hole at the top, clear the hole with a fine knitting needle or similar.) Leave it to dry for a minute and then peel off the masking tape.

3 APPLYING THE CRAYON LINES

Before you begin to add the crayon lines to the pepper shaker, drop a fine knitting needle or similar object into the central hole. This will allow you to decorate the pot without touching it with your fingers and accidentally smudging the paint. Use the colored crayons to draw stripes following the pencil marks. It is easiest to draw your lines down from the top to the bottom. Apply colored stripes to the base of the salt shaker in the same way.

4 APPLYING THE GLAZE

Apply a coat of glaze to the pepper shaker and to the crayoned base of the salt shaker only. It may help to dab on the glaze rather than using long brush strokes. If you see the crayon lines beginning to lift, stop and re-load the brush with glaze. Alternatively, the pepper shaker can be dipped into a bucket of clear glaze. The shakers are now ready for firing.

Acrylic painting

Not suitable.

Salt & pepper shakers

Although they are a pair, salt and pepper shakers don't need to look exactly the same. It is actually quite useful to be able to discriminate between them at a glance, as shown in these illustrations.

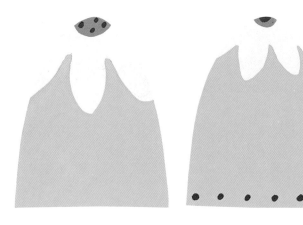

1 Resist out the different-sized flowers with masking fluid, and paint the backgrounds yellow. Remove the masking fluid. Paint on the purple dots.

2 Paint the straight and squiggly lines with masking fluid, and fill in the background with purple paint. Peel off the masking fluid.

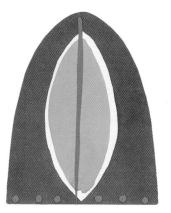

3 Draw the shields, then paint them. Paint the background colors, leaving haloes around the shields. Add green lines, dots, and zigzags.

4 Stick masking tape on the shakers, leaving a band around the base of each. Paint the green bands. Remove the tape. Mono-print the leaves.

5 Paint thick blue stripes fanning out from the top of the salt shaker, and dab dots the same color on the pepper shaker.

Egg cups

Because egg cups are so small, the simpler your design, the more dramatic the overall effect. It is also hard work concentrating on objects of this size for any length of time. If you have a set of egg cups, you might like to come up with a theme. You could paint each cup with a different bird, such as a chicken, duck, or quail, or paint all the cups in the same pattern but in a selection of colors.

1 Paint both egg cups free-style, starting with the lightest colors and progressing through to the darkest color.

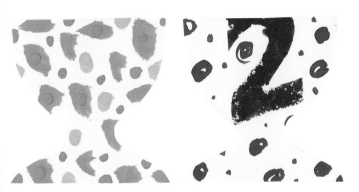

2 left: Dab on pale blue paint, followed by darker blue. Paint the taupe dots. right: Stencil the number 2. Paint the squirls and dots.

3 left: Paint the egg cup orange. Use an underglaze pen or paint for the hen. right: Paint the egg cup purple. Sgraffito the spirals, stripes, and dots.

4 left: Paint the egg cup pink. Mono-print the shell. Paint the rim and dashes dark pink. right: Paint the rose and leaves. Highlight with underglaze pencil.

5 Paint both egg cups free-style, starting with the palest colors and finishing with the darkest. Leave a halo around the dots on the rim.

Project templates

These templates are for the projects featured on pages 38, 44, 52, 64, and 70. Please refer to pages 24–25 for instructions on how to use them.

Floral teapot

Bird pitcher

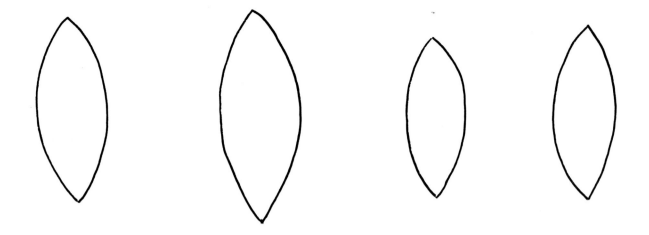

Africa mug

Fish plate

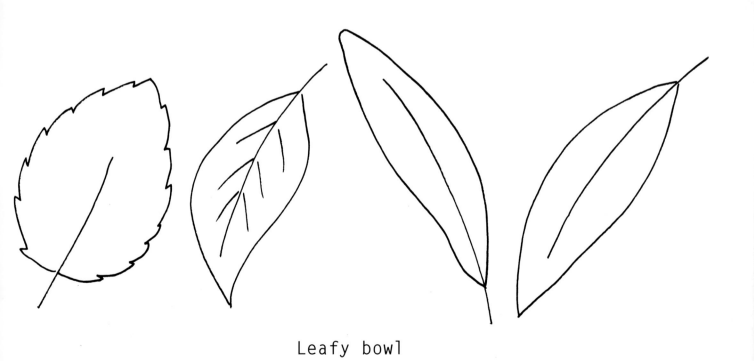

Leafy bowl

Alternative motifs

These motifs – some of which you will recognize from the alternative artwork designs – are intended as inspirational starting points for your own designs, although they can be traced and used as they are, or enlarged or reduced on a photocopier (see pages 24–25). The gray washes are only a guide to help you decide how to apply the color. The actual outlines can be used for making stencils or stamps, or for copying with an underglaze pen or pencil.

Flowers

Fish

Shells

Leaves

Birds

Fruit & vegetables

Letters & numbers

ABCDE   ABCDE
FGHIJK   FGHIJK
LMNOP   LMNOP
QRSTU   QRSTU
VWXYZ   VWXYZ

abcde   abcde
fghijklm   fghijklm
nopqrst   nopqrst
uvwxyz   uvwxyz
01234   01234
56789   56789

Published in the United
States by
Laurel Glen Publishing
An imprint of the Advantage
Publishers Group
5880 Oberlin Drive,
San Diego, CA 92121-4794
www.advantagebooksonline.com

First published in 2000
by Conran Octopus Limited

All notations of errors or
omissions should be
addressed to Laurel Glen
Publishing, editorial
department, at the above
address. All other
correspondence (author
inquiries, permissions and
rights) concerning the
content of this book should
be addressed to:
Conran Octopus Limited
2-4 Heron Quays
London E14 4JP

ISBN 1 57145 669 4

Library of Congress
Cataloging-in-Publication
Data available upon request

Printed in China

ACKNOWLEDGMENTS

Author's acknowledgments
I would like to thank my
husband, parents and mother-in-
law for all the help and
support they have given me
during the creation of this
book, and also George for being
such a good boy. A special
thank you to Pottery Crafts for
supplying materials for the
projects featured in this book,
and to Potclays and Kevin
Millward Ceramics (see below).

Publisher's acknowledgments
The publisher would like to
thank Claudia Dulak, Alison
Bolus and Kathie Gill.

This listing contains internet-
accessible businesses that may
be able to supply some of the
items used in this book.
However, inclusion on this list
does not constitute an
endorsement of the supplier or
their products by the
publisher.

American Ceramic Society
Ceramic Information Center
735 Ceramic Place
Westerville, OH 43081-8720
http://www.acers.org

**National Council on Education
for the Ceramic Arts**
1-800-99-NCECA

SUPPLIERS

A.R.T. Studio Clay Company
9320 Michigan Ave.
Sturtevant, WI 53177-2425
877-ART-CLAY
http://www.artclay.com

Arnels Ceramic Molds
2330 SE Harney St.
Portland, OR 97202
503-236-8540
http://www.arnels.com

Big Ceramics Store
http://www.bigceramicsstore.com

Ceramic King
3300 Girard Ave.
Albuquerque, NM 87107
800-781-2529
http://www.nmclay.com

Clay in Motion
Rte. 3 Box 120 A
Walla Walla, WA 99362
509-529-6146
http://www.clayinmotion.com

The Clay Studio
139 N. Second St.
Philadelphia, PA 19106
215-925-3453
http://www.theclaystudio.com

Double Nickel Ceramics
Frank Gleasons Molds
1212 West US Highway 24
Independence, MO 64050
816-252-5174
http://www.doublenickel.com

Mayco Colors
Columbus, OH
http://www.maycocolors.com

Minnesota Clay
800-252-9872
http://www.mm.com/mnclayus/

Sheffield Pottery
US Rte. 7 Box 399
Sheffield, MA 01257
888-SPI-CLAY
http://www.sheffield-
pottery.com

POTTERY CAFES

Adventures in Ceramics
PO Box 1602
Brookfield, WI
262-790-5199
http://www.adventuresinceramics.
com

Ceramic Art Space
12532 Riverside Dr.
Valley Village, VA 91607
818-752-9767

The Clayroom
1408 Beacon St.
Brookline, MA
617-566-7575
http://www.clayroom.com

Color Me Mine
Locations nationally
http://www.colormemine.com

Glazenfyre
Virginia Beach, VA
757-464-2800
http://www.glazenfyre.com

The Painted Pot
333 Smith St.
Brooklyn, NY
717-222-0334
http://www.paintedpot.com

Pottery Potentials
5 Post Office Ave.
Andover, MA 01810
978-475-6113
http://www.potterypotentials.com

Puttin on the Paint
2501 W. Colorado Ave.
Colorado Springs, CO 80904
719-633-5330
http://www.puttinonthepaint.com

Studio You
2495 Lee Blvd.
Cleveland Heights, OH 044118
218-321-7211
http://www.studioyou.com

Terra Mia
4037 24th St.
San Francisco, CA
415-642-9911
http://www.terramia.net

Youre Fired
6925 Orchard Lake Rd.
Boardwalk Mall
W. Bloomfield, MI 48322
248-851-5594
http://www.yourefired.com